Jellybean

D0326105

Story written by Gill Munton
Illustrated by Tim Archbold

St. Joseph's Primary School
Commerell Street
Greenwich SE10 9AN

Speed Sounds

Consonants *Ask children to say the sounds.*

f	l	m	n	r	s	v	z	sh	th	ng
ff	ll	mm	nn	rr	ss	(ve)	zz			nk
ph	le	mb	kn	wr	(se)		(se)			
					ce		s			

b	c	d	g	h	j	p	(qu)	t	w	x	y	ch
bb	k	dd	gg		g	pp		tt	wh			tch
	ck				ge							

Each box contains one sound but sometimes more than one grapheme.
*Focus graphemes for this story are **circled**.*

Vowels

Ask your child to say the sounds in and out of order.

a	e ea	i	o	u	ay a͡-e	ee ea y e	igh i͡-e ie i	ow o͡-e o
at	hen	in	on	up	day	see	high	blow

oo u͡-e ue	oo	ar	or oor ore	air are	ir ur er	ou	oy oi
zoo	look	car	for	fair	whirl	shout	boy

5

Story Green Words

Ask children to read the words first in Fred Talk and then say the word.

seal   beast   hay   cream   leave   mouse   cage   cheap   noise

wolf*

Ask children to say the syllables and then read the whole word.

Jelly bean   wea sel   greedy   afford   gold fish   fright en

---

Ask children to read the root first and then the whole word with the suffix.

crease → creased   freak → freaked   tease → teased

bleat → bleated   squeak → squeaked   scream → screamed

* Challenge Words

Vocabulary Check

Discuss the meaning (as used in the story) after the children have read each word.

	definition:	sentence:
seal	show the picture on page 9 to explain what a seal looks like	Please let me have a pet seal!
creased	crumpled and wrinkled	An elephant with creased grey skin.
freaked	went crazy	Mum freaked out at first, but then she got me one.
hay	dried long grass	We had to feed it three sacks of hay.
bleated	the noise a sheep makes	The sheep bleated and bleated.
frighten her out of her wits	make her really, really scared	The fish is cheap and doesn't frighten her out of her wits

Red Words

Ask children to practise reading the words across the rows, down the columns and in and out of order clearly and quickly.

any	what	one	was
want	does	could	said
some	of	who	brother
there	their	I'm	could
all	who	where	two

Jellybean

"Please, please, please, Mum, let me have a pet!
A horse or a bee or a duck or a seal,
a wolf or a weasel, a flea or an eel –
any pet will do!"

At least, that's what I said.
But what I really wanted was ... an elephant.
An elephant with creased grey skin
and a trunk as thick as a tree.

Mum freaked out at first,
but she got me one.

We kept it in the garden.
It was a bit of a squash, what with
Dad's beans and Dean's go-kart.

We had to feed that greedy beast
three sacks of hay each morning.
Mum said we couldn't afford it,
and the elephant had to leave.

"Please, please, please, Mum, let me have a pet!

A horse or a bee or a duck or a seal,

a wolf or a weasel, a flea or an eel —

any pet will do!"

At least, that's what I said.
But what I really wanted was ...
a sheep.
A sheep, with long yellow
teeth and soft, cream wool.

Mum teased me about it at first,

but she got me one.

We let the sheep sleep in the kitchen.

It bleated – and bleated

– and then bleated some more.

It bleated all night, and no one got any sleep.

So the sheep had to leave.

"Please, please, please, Mum, let me have a pet!

A horse or a bee or a duck or a seal,

a wolf or a weasel, a flea or an eel –

any pet will do!"

At least, that's what I said.

But what I really wanted was ... a mouse.

A sweet little mouse, with neat pink feet.

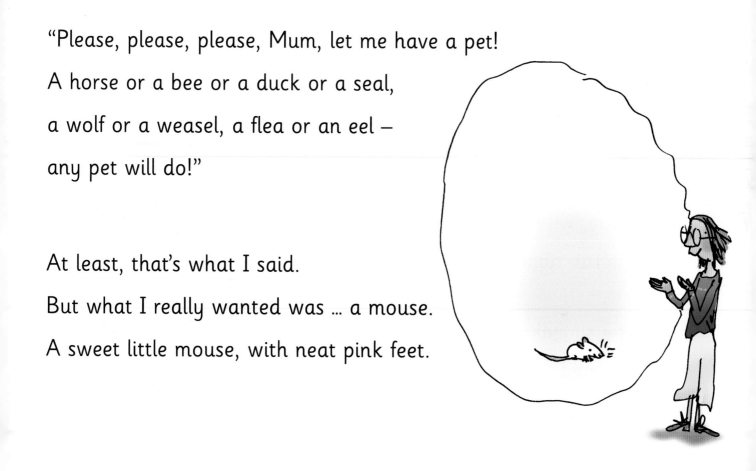

Mum wasn't too keen at first, but she got me one.

Its cage was easy to keep clean.
It liked eating bits of cheese.

But one day, when Mum was cleaning her teeth,
the mouse ran right up the leg of her jeans!

The mouse squeaked.
Mum screamed.
And the mouse – had to leave.
Fast.

"Please, please, please, Mum, let me have a pet!

A horse or a bee or a duck or a seal,

a wolf or a weasel, a flea or an eel –

any pet will do!"

That's what I said.

And what I got was – a goldfish.

I've called it Jellybean.

Mum says that it's cheap to feed, it doesn't make a noise –

and it doesn't frighten her out of her wits!

Questions to talk about

Ask children to TTYP each question using 'Fastest finger' (FF) or 'Have a think' (HaT).

p.9 (FF) What does she like about elephants?

p.10 (FF) How many sacks of hay did they have to feed the elephant each morning?

p.11 (FF) What does she like about sheep?

p.12 (FF) What did the sheep do all night?

p.13 (FF) What does she like about mice?

p.14 (FF) What happened while Mum was cleaning her teeth?

p.15 (HaT) Why might she have named her goldfish Jellybean? What do you think?

Questions to read and answer

(Children complete without your help.)

1. What was the first pet that the child really wanted?

2. Was an elephant a good pet? Why?

3. Why did the mouse have to leave?

4. Why does mum get a fish?

5. What pet would you like? Why?

Speedy Green Words

Ask children to practise reading the words across the rows, down the columns and in and out of order clearly and quickly.

please	really	least	leave
make	please	about	morning
have	horse	yellow	teeth
pink	feet	frighten	night
sleep	with	first	sweet